Things a father need his daughters to know

Santiego Rivers

Before I close my eyes, I want to come to terms with my past and be contemptuous with my life today. I am far from perfect, but I am stepping towards my salvation.

Before I close my eyes, I need you to know that my heart, love, and prayers were always present, even in my absence.

Sometimes being the father that a man wishes he could be becomes overshadowed by his **pride, fears**, and **anger** of the man he used to be.

I have allowed my **pride, fears**, and **anger** to take precious moments away from my life that I will never be able to get back.

So, I am writing this book to give back all the knowledge that a father would want his Goddess to have.

You are what inspires a male to want to become a **Man**. For your acceptance, I have always tried to become a **Better Man**.

All the **hate** and **anger** you may have towards me, please allow me to carry those burdens so that your heart and soul can be free.

I pray that this book will be the first step that allows us to be as close as I have always wished that we could be.

Before I close my eyes

Things that a father needs his daughters to know

Copyright © 2021 by **Santiego Rivers**

All rights reserved. This book may not be reproduced or transmitted in any form without the author's written permission.

"no copyright infringement is intended."

ISBN 978-1-7370516-8-8

Table of Content

Chanice Cowart (Pgs.6-16)

Genesis Serrano (Pgs. 17-25)

Diamond Rivers (Pgs. 26-28)

Isis Hughes (Pgs. 29-34)

My closing words (Pgs. 35-36)

Chanice Cowart

All men are not dogs. Sometimes they just need the right inspiration to want to understand.

Chanice, your mom was the inspiration that made me want to be the best man I could be.

We met when we both were in high school. I saw your mom walking down the hall, and her smile touched my soul.

Your mom was and is a "Natural" beautiful woman. I followed her in the classroom to get to know her.

I saw that she was pregnant, but I did not care. I was hooked on her! We talked, and our conversation made me want to know more about her.

Your mother was as beautiful on the inside as she was outside. My nickname for your mother was **"Swelly"** because she was pregnant with you when we met.

I don't remember all the details of our time together, but I know it was special.

Your mother came into my life during a time when I thought that my life would be coming to an end soon, courtesy of me.

I had no plans of living past eighteen years of age during that time in my life. I did not know why I was given life or my life purpose.

All I am and hopefully will ever be is because the Most High brought you and your mother into my life.

Your mother and I spent a lot of time together. Even when we were not together, we talked on the phone a lot.

I used to go to the doctor's appointments with her, and I was even fortunate to be there when you officially came into the world.

Your birth is the only birth that I had the pleasure of witnessing my children. It was an honor to have that experience.

Meeting your mother allowed me the pleasure of meeting the rest of your family. Your grandmother, **Beverly Stewart,** was very special to my life.

She helped to mold and shape me in many ways. She helped me get closer to my mother.

Your grandmother set a high bar for any mothers-in-law that I will ever have. Although I never married your mother, I did have the pleasure of having her as my fiancé.

We got engaged when I came back from college. I will tell you more about that later. But, first, let me tell you more about our high school years.

Chivon and I went to my prom together. I had no plans to go, but I think your grandmother talked me into going.

She may have the pictures of our prom. She allowed me to drive her car to prom. There are two main reasons I didn't want to go to prom.

My first reason: The school we went to was not my favorite. I came from the south side of town, and the school was located on the north side of town. After all the athletic accomplishments that I did at the school, I felt they never respected me. As a result, I have not been to one class reunion.

My second reason: I cannot dance. You may find it a little funny when you finish reading the rest of my book. I think that your mother and I only danced to slow songs at prom that night.

At some point, I had moved in with your family before I went off to college. It allowed me to get closer to you and your mother.

While Chivon was pregnant with you, I remember rubbing her belly, talking to you, and fussing at you when you kicked.

Getting closer to you made it hard for me to leave and go off to school. While I was off at school, Chivon and I would talk for hours on the phone.

Your grandmother had the high phone bill to prove it. We both missed each other, and I missed you.

I feared that my being away from you would make you forget all about me.

When I came home from college for Christmas break, I came home to you and your mother. I was very excited!

We spent a lot of time together during my break. It felt like a real family.

Your mother would cook for me and wash my clothes. She did everything that showed a man he was loved and respected by his woman. She set the bar high for any woman to follow, so she was the first woman that I asked to bear my last name.

An unfortunate situation happened when I went back to school, which allowed me the pleasure of coming back home to you and your mother for good.

Again, we were all a happy family in your grandmother's house. Me, your mother, your auntie, and you all slept in the same room.

It was crazy, but we made it work. There were many nights that your auntie **Nuavia** slept on the couch.

Your uncle **Ted** had his room for himself. I loved **Nuavia** and your Uncle **Ted**. They were both extraordinary and unique people.

I wish that I had the pleasure of being in their life longer to have helped them through the situations in life that they faced.

I regret not being in your life longer to fill any void or emptiness within your heart. A girl should always have a father in her life to model how a man should treat a woman.

The first thing a man should do is make sure that he put the Most High first. Any union or plan that does not have the blessing of the Most High will surely fail.

I am not a religious person, but I am a faithful and obedient spiritual being who worships the Most High.

The second thing a man should do is love his daughters for better or worse. Having a daughter will bring him closer to his emotions and feelings.

When a man loves, he wants to protect that which he loves. A man protects by setting rules and guidelines to live by, but unfortunately, his daughters make him say yes even when he should say no.

Having a father in your life helps a young girl learn to choose a mate based upon their father's standards.

Watching her father, a young girl sees how affectionate he is with the mother and all the little things a man does to show his love.

A man closes and opens doors for his woman. He buys her flowers just because it is Tuesday. He is slow to anger and quick to give.

A man is a provider, and even when he can't provide the way he wants, he finds ways to help the family.

A man will go without so that the family will always have. A man plans for tomorrow so that the family will be okay today.

A man is not perfect, but a woman and his family will inspire him to try his best to meet that standard.

I will not sit here and tell you what type of man I was to you and your mother; that is a conversation you must have with her.

I can tell you that not having you in my life made my life a living hell. Being without you has affected my life in many ways. Letting my pride take me out of your life made me want to become a father because I didn't have you in my life anymore.

I admit that I struggled to be a father to my kids, maybe because I was missing you out of my life. It's hard to be without the people who inspired you to want to live.

I have often asked myself this question; How could I truly be happy when my heart has always been with you and your mother.

When you truly love someone and give them not only your heart but also a piece of your soul, it makes it hard to love anyone else truly.

Here's a weird thought. The strange thing that makes me pause and think is this:

I **never** wanted kids, but I have always wanted you in my life. (I say again) I **never** wanted kids, but I have always wanted you in my life.

This whole book could be about you and what you mean to my life, *"Chicken Hawk."* But, instead, I must let your sister know what they also mean to my life.

I called you "Chicken Hawk" because I used to feed you chicken nuggets all the time. I loved watching you eat them with your little hands and two teeth.

Genesis & Sabrina

I met your mother at a club that I used to work at. I was a male entertainer. Basically, I was a stripper.

Although I was not old enough to be in the club, I still performed there on certain nights. I also worked as a teacher aide and a wrestling coach in the school system.

Your aunt got me to dance with your mother for her birthday, at the club I was working at.

My stage name was *Teddy Bare*. **Beverly Stewart** helped me to come up with my stage name, and **Chivon Cowart** was one of the people who helped me learn how to dance.

Your mother and I would meet again in Ybor City. I was there with my friend **Charles**, and **your mother** was there with her people.

I did not like being in Ybor. I am a homebody, as you know. It was my friend **Charles's** idea to go there.

Your mom and her friends followed me in Ybor. I was scared at first. But, eventually, we did talk and hit it off.

One of the many things that I love about your mom is that she is the opposite of me. But, ironically, over the years, I have also learned that she reminds me of my mother.

Men are attracted to women who have similar traits as their mothers, and Women are attracted to men who have similar characteristics to their fathers.

You also have those people with mommy and daddy not being in the picture issues, so it is important to have kids with people who will stick around no matter what.

My mental state was not where it should have been when I met your mother. I was still hurting from my last relationship, and I would have my first biological child with a woman I did not know.

Your mother's lifestyle was crazy, but it was the distraction that I needed in my life. She was always going out to the clubs, but I only wanted to go to the club when I was working at them.

I did not start drinking until I met your mother. She and your uncles used to make fun of me for drinking virgin strawberry daiquiri's.

I would eventually meet **Sely/ Genesis** once **your mother** and I got closer. **Sely** was a beautiful lady with a lot of energy.

It seemed that we got along at first, but unfortunately, we had some rocky years together.

She had some stubborn ways, and I wasn't brave enough not to let my stubbornness come out of me.

I wanted to be closer to her because I felt that we could help each other grow as people.

I never felt comfortable in the relationship with your mother. Although I loved her very much, we never could seem to make it work to walk down the aisle as man and wife.

I did propose to her because I wanted us to be a real family, but unfortunately, I never had that pleasure.

I was afraid that your mother would go back to your biological father for most of our relationship since they had been together for so long.

For many years I don't think your grandmother liked me that much. I would later feel different late into my union with **your mother**.

Your mother and I had been together for almost twenty years, off and on. We have been through many ups and downs.

We argued, in the beginning, a lot over you, **Sely**. I regret not being man enough to do whatever it took to make sure you were happy.

A real man learns to swallow his pride for the people he loves. But, **Sely,** it was you and your mother who taught me that hard lesson.

It took longer than I wished it did because it cost me a lot of time out of you and your sister's life.

I never wanted you two to be raised in a family where the parents always fought and split up.

I wanted to set a better example for both of you. I regret the lifestyle that I lived during that time.

I wanted to be a person that you both could be proud of. So, I kept trying to make things work with your mother for two reasons.

The first reason is that I was in love with her. You don't spend twenty years with someone that you do not love. She is my weakness.

The second reason is that I wanted a family. I wanted you both to grow up with a man in the house.

I never had the honor of having a dad in the house, so I wanted you and your sister to have it.

Sely, I feel that our relationship got better late in the years; I apologize for taking so long.

There was so much that I wanted to teach you, but I did not know if you wanted to learn them from me.

You are your mother's child, and we come from a different culture. Your grandmother raised your mother to be a certain way, and I did not know if that were the path you would take.

For the most part, I noticed that you still do what Sely wants. So, I pray that it is working out for you and you are happy with the direction that your life is headed?

My love for you will never change. The man that I have become is because of you. It damn sure was not easy, but it was worth it.

I am genuinely sorry for whatever I did to take you out of my life. One minute, you were the only one there, and the next minute you were gone.

If it was about the Mazda, I wished we could have been adults and talked about it. But, remember, I am the one who bought you your first car and co-signed for you when no one else would.

Regardless of how you feel about me, I would still get out of bed and come to you whenever you need me.

The door to my heart will always be open to you

Sabrina/"Birdy,"

You have always been my world. I get speechless when I think about everything you mean to me.

You have always had a good heart and soul. I would move mountains and part seas to keep a smile on your face.

I never wanted not to be a part of your life. I wanted to be there for your first steps, and the day you walked down the aisle.

Your first steps were at Chuck E Cheese

You saw and heard all the excitement, and it made you start walking. We used to go there a lot.

I was lucky enough to share the early parts of your childhood, but I missed out on the crucial years of your life.

For twenty years, I fought to be a part of your life so that you would know that I desperately wanted to be there.

One of the weaknesses that made me a lousy father was that I didn't know how to tell the people I loved that I was hurting.

I felt that you and your sister didn't want me around, so it made it easy not to be around.

You all would go on trips and vacations, and I was never invited. Of course, there was plenty of girls' trip, but what about the family?

These things are not your fault. I could have spoken up or done something to try and change things around.

I am just heartbroken that we have no type of communication. I pray that you are doing well and that your life is heading in the direction you want it to go.

I know that your mother will always be there for you, and her family will be there also.

My door will always be open to you. I pray that you will one day forgive me for whatever I did to make you walk out the door.

Isis

I want the world for you, but I understand that it will never occur if you don't want it for yourself, no matter how bad I want this for you.

You are the only child that I had the pleasure to help name. I picked the name Isis because it has meaning and purpose.

I had made you tapes as a child to understand better where your name came from.

We spent a lot of your early life together. Your mom made it all possible. As a result, your mom was one of the few women I pursued.

I loved your mother, and I still consider her a friend. But, unfortunately, we never had the pleasure of playing house together.

We met each other at the wrong time in our lives. **Monica** is a good woman. All my daughter's moms are good people. Unfortunately, I never had the pleasure of being in a relationship with my son's mother, so I can't attest to her character.

Like I did for your sister **Sabrina**, I started teaching you early to prepare for school. I put you on a routine.

We spent a lot of time together. I wanted to raise you in the ways that I did not truly have a chance to raise your siblings.

With me being at a transitioning point in my life, my money did not allow me to have you live with me as long as I would have liked for you to.

I was finishing my career as a male entertainer, trying to become a certified teacher.

I was in college and thought about going to law school. But, I decided to become a teacher instead.

I didn't have help to raise you on my own so, you mainly lived with your mom out of town.

The one thing that I was afraid of was that when you left my house, you would lose all the skills that I was teaching you.

Living with me, I ensured that you were doing all the things you needed to do. You had your chores, your homework, and your bedtime. You had these things to do before you even started school.

I noticed the difference every time you came to spend time with me. It seemed that I always had to get you back on track.

I was fortunate enough to have you at my wedding. So, I wanted your siblings to share in a moment like this.

I desired to have you come live with **Somone & me.** I wanted you to experience how a family should operate. I wanted you to see the little things that family does that matter the most.

 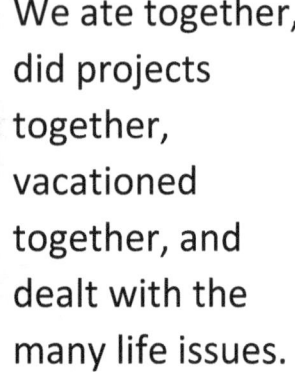

We ate together, did projects together, vacationed together, and dealt with the many life issues.

We were not perfect, but we could have made it work if we had given it enough time together.

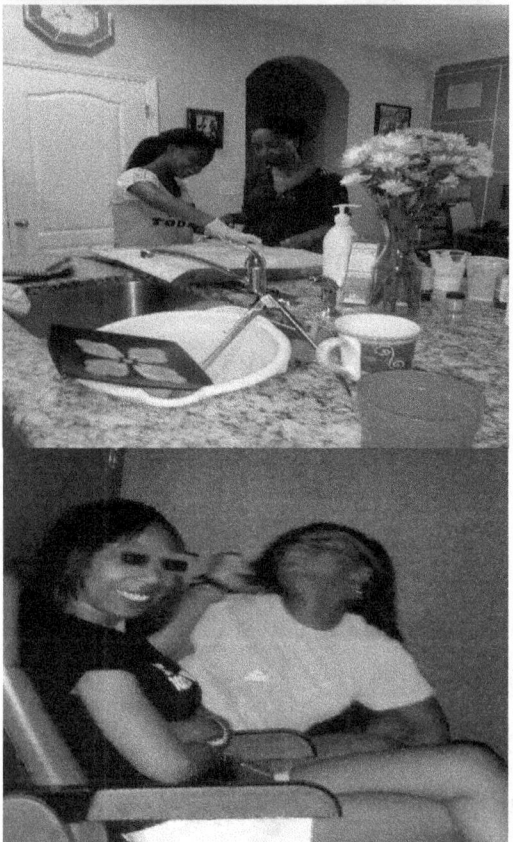

It did not help matters out going through the Covid-19 pandemic.

Plus, I dealt with medical issues that put me in the ICU twice. I am still struggling with my medical issues. **Isis**, you are probably the sibling struggling with the same problems I struggled with the most.

I will do all the things that I need to so that I can help you through this stage/phase in your life. But, you must do your part too.

I know that you are _13 going on 30_, but you are still a child who needs guidance and a father, including love.

So, that you know, I do not need your permission to be your father; I just am. This statement goes for all my children.

Isis, I hope that there is time to reach you before it is too late. I want us to get close again, so I will step up and do my part.

I love you regardless of who you like. Nothing will change the way that I feel about you. I have been hated before.

Things that a father needs his daughters to know

No man is perfect, but the Most High. The people you love will hurt you, disappoint you, and let you down.

They will also go out of their way to make things right between the both of you.

Never judge a person by the mistakes that they make. Instead, judge a person by their willingness to make things right when they make their mistake.

Most of you have been around me long enough to know my character and soul as a man.

If you gave me a chance, you would see that I am only getting better every day as a person.

It is not my place to judge you for your choices in your life. However, I have my cross to bear.

I will listen, understand, and be honest when you ask my opinion. But, as you already know, I will not lose my cool regardless of the situation.

I have learned over time that life will teach us lessons whether we are prepared or not. You are the ones that will have to live with the decisions that you make. Let go of your anger.

If you feel that I have wronged you in any way. Let us make time to talk about it, so I may apologize to you and help you release that pain.

They say that time heals all wounds. I just want to make sure that your wounds heal properly.

I stand ready, willing, and able to do all that I can to be a part of your life once again. I just want a relationship with you all.

Chickenhawk, Sely, Birdy, and Swiper, I love you all!!!

I wrote this book as an opportunity for my daughters could get to know me better. I did not write this book to attack or slander anyone.

I am grateful for all the people who came into my life and served a purpose that helped me become a better man.

I would not be the man I am today without you being a part of my life. So please don't allow this book to make you feel any other way but appreciated, even if you did not feel that way in our union.

Time heals all wounds, so I pray that your life is filled with the happiness and joy you deserve.

Thank you for reading my book and being the inspiration I needed to become a better man!

Having love and joy in your life will make all the pain you have been through worth it.

www.ingramcontent.com/pod-product-compliance
Lightning Source LLC
Chambersburg PA
CBHW071339190426
43193CB00042B/2043